SureShot Books
PUBLISHING LLC

Books have the power to change lives.

SureShot Books Publishing LLC is part of the SureShot 2k family of companies that was founded in 1990 to help inmates & their families by making it possible to improve their lives with the Power of Reading.

Here at SureShot Books, we fervently believe that the fact that you have made a mistake does and should not mean that your life is ruined forever.

We believe that everyone deserves a second chance.

Contact Us with any questions or concerns:
SureShot Books Publishing LLC
P.O. Box 924, Nyack, New York 10960
845.675.7505
Email Us:
info@sureshotbooks.com

SureShot Books

PUBLISHING LLC

**Books have the POWER
to change lives!**

INMATE NAME:

INMATE NUMBER:

CONTACT INFO

NAME:

ADDRESS:

PHONE: NOTE:

EMAIL: WEBSITE:

NAME:

ADDRESS:

PHONE: NOTE:

EMAIL: WEBSITE:

NAME:

ADDRESS:

PHONE: NOTE:

EMAIL: WEBSITE:

NAME:

ADDRESS:

PHONE: NOTE:

EMAIL: WEBSITE:

CONTACT INFO

NAME: _____

ADDRESS: _____

_____

PHONE: _____ NOTE: _____

EMAIL: _____ WEBSITE: _____

NAME: _____

ADDRESS: _____

_____

PHONE: _____ NOTE: _____

EMAIL: _____ WEBSITE: _____

NAME: _____

ADDRESS: _____

_____

PHONE: _____ NOTE: _____

EMAIL: _____ WEBSITE: _____

NAME: _____

ADDRESS: _____

_____

PHONE: _____ NOTE: _____

EMAIL: _____ WEBSITE: _____

CONTACT INFO

NAME: _____

ADDRESS: _____

PHONE: _____ NOTE: _____

EMAIL: _____ WEBSITE: _____

NAME: _____

ADDRESS: _____

PHONE: _____ NOTE: _____

EMAIL: _____ WEBSITE: _____

NAME: _____

ADDRESS: _____

PHONE: _____ NOTE: _____

EMAIL: _____ WEBSITE: _____

NAME: _____

ADDRESS: _____

PHONE: _____ NOTE: _____

EMAIL: _____ WEBSITE: _____

CONTACT INFO

NAME:

ADDRESS:

PHONE: NOTE:

EMAIL: WEBSITE:

NAME:

ADDRESS:

PHONE: NOTE:

EMAIL: WEBSITE:

NAME:

ADDRESS:

PHONE: NOTE:

EMAIL: WEBSITE:

NAME:

ADDRESS:

PHONE: NOTE:

EMAIL: WEBSITE:

Year At A Glance:

January

February

March

April

May

June

Year At A Glance:

July

August

September

October

November

December

This journal is a journey of self-discovery, growth, and empowerment—a space where you can set goals, dream big, and find purpose through the experiences you wish to accomplish. We believe that every dream, no matter how big or small, holds the potential to inspire and transform your life.

Life's journey may have brought you to a place of temporary separation from your loved ones, but it has also presented you with an opportunity to explore new horizons, connect with your passions, and discover the immense power within you. This journal is a testament to the boundless potential that resides in every individual, regardless of circumstances.

In these pages, you have the freedom to dream without limitations—to envision a life that fills your heart with joy, purpose, and fulfillment. Embrace the magic of setting goals that challenge and excite you, as each goal becomes a stepping stone on the path to self-discovery and personal growth.

By crafting your bucket list and immersing yourself in the experiences you dream of, you open doors to endless possibilities. These experiences, no matter how simple or grand, will leave an indelible mark on your journey, creating cherished memories and life lessons that will stay with you forever.

Dreaming big is an act of courage, and we applaud you for embracing this journey of self-exploration. The dreams you hold dear will light your path even during the darkest hours, serving as beacons of hope and inspiration.

As you write in this journal, remember that your dreams matter, and your aspirations are worthy of pursuit. Through this process, you will gain insights into your passions, strengths, and the incredible potential within you. Embrace the journey with an open heart, and know that each step you take brings you closer to a future filled with purpose, fulfillment, and a sense of achievement.

May the "Dream Big: Inmate's Bucket List Journal" be your companion, guide, and confidant on this extraordinary expedition. Trust in your dreams, take bold strides, and remember that the power to transform your life lies within you.

With excitement and anticipation,

Tips

Writing a bucket list is an exciting and empowering process that allows you to identify your dreams, aspirations, and goals. Here are some tips and advice to help you create a meaningful and inspiring bucket list:

Reflect on Your Passions and Interests: Start by thinking about the things that ignite your passion and interest. What activities, experiences, or places have you always wanted to explore?

Embrace both Short-term and Long-term Goals: Include a mix of short-term goals that you can achieve relatively quickly and long-term goals that may require more planning and effort.

Be Specific and Detailed: Instead of general ideas, make your bucket list items specific and detailed. For example, instead of "Travel more," specify destinations you want to visit.

Set Realistic and Achievable Goals: While it's essential to dream big, ensure your goals are realistic and attainable within your resources and capabilities.

Step Out of Your Comfort Zone: Use your bucket list to challenge yourself and step out of your comfort zone. Consider activities that push your boundaries and help you grow.

Tips

Prioritize What Matters Most: Rank your bucket list items based on what matters most to you. This will help you focus on the experiences that align with your values and aspirations.

Include Different Categories: Organize your bucket list into categories such as travel, personal development, hobbies, relationships, or charitable endeavors.

Consider Different Time Frames: Some goals may be achieved within a year, while others may take a lifetime. Be mindful of different time frames for each item.

Seek Inspiration: Draw inspiration from books, movies, documentaries, or people who have accomplished remarkable feats. Use their stories to fuel your own aspirations.

Collaborate with Loved Ones: Share your bucket list with family and friends. Consider creating shared goals or involving them in some of your experiences.

Revisit and Revise: Your bucket list is a living document. Revisit it regularly, cross off achieved goals, and add new ones as your interests and priorities evolve.

Celebrate Your Accomplishments: Celebrate every milestone and achievement on your bucket list. Acknowledge your progress and the growth that comes with each experience.

Tips

Be Open to Change: Life is full of surprises, and your aspirations may evolve over time. Stay open to new opportunities and be willing to adapt your bucket list accordingly.

Start Now: Don't wait for the perfect moment to begin. Start taking small steps towards your goals today, and let the journey unfold naturally.

Embrace the Journey: Remember that the purpose of a bucket list is not just about ticking off items; it's about embracing the journey, gaining experiences, and finding joy in the pursuit of your dreams.

Writing a bucket list is a personal and meaningful endeavor. It reflects your hopes, passions, and desires. Let it be a source of inspiration, motivation, and a reminder to make the most of every moment life offers. Dream big, take action, and savor the experiences that enrich your life.

Examples:

Travel and Adventure:

Visit a famous landmark or historical site.
Take a scenic road trip and explore new places.
Go camping and connect with nature.
Try an adventurous activity like skydiving or zip-lining.
Take a hot air balloon ride and see the world from above.

Learning and Personal Growth:

Earn a degree or certification in a subject of interest.
Learn a new language and practice conversing with others.
Take up a creative hobby like painting, writing, or playing an instrument.
Attend workshops or seminars on topics that intrigue you.
Read a book from different genres and expand your knowledge.

Fitness and Health:

Run a marathon or participate in a local race.
Take up yoga or meditation for mental and physical well-being.
Try a new sport or fitness activity, such as rock climbing or martial arts.
Set a fitness goal, like achieving a specific number of push-ups or pull-ups.
Adopt a healthier diet and experiment with new nutritious recipes.

Examples:

Relationships and Connections:

Reconnect with old friends through letters or phone calls.
Strengthen family bonds by writing letters to loved ones regularly.
Make new friends by participating in social activities or support groups.
Express gratitude and appreciation to the people who have supported you.
Rekindle a broken relationship through understanding and forgiveness.

Giving Back and Helping Others:

Volunteer for a charitable organization or a cause you believe in.
Donate books, artwork, or other creations to benefit others.
Share your knowledge or skills by mentoring or tutoring fellow inmates.
Participate in prison programs that support rehabilitation and growth.
Write letters of encouragement to fellow inmates or those in need.

Examples:

Overcoming Challenges:

Attend therapy or counseling to work through past traumas.
Practice mindfulness and meditation to manage stress and anxiety.
Develop coping mechanisms for handling difficult emotions.
Engage in self-reflection to understand personal strengths and weaknesses.
Set a goal to overcome a specific fear or limitation.

Future Planning:

Create a detailed plan for post-release goals and aspirations.
Research potential career paths or entrepreneurial ventures.
Consider educational opportunities or vocational training for future success.
Develop financial planning skills to ensure a stable future.
Write a letter to your future self, envisioning the life you want to lead.

Remember that a bucket list is a deeply personal journey. Tailor it to your unique interests and aspirations. It's a roadmap to self-discovery, growth, and fulfillment, guiding you towards a life that aligns with your values and passions. Dream big, embrace challenges, and make the most of every opportunity that comes your way.

"The only limit to our realization of tomorrow will be our doubts of today." - Franklin D. Roosevelt

"BELIEVE YOU CAN, AND YOU'RE HALFWAY THERE." - THEODORE ROOSEVEL

Guide:

Travel and Adventure:

List three countries or cities you want to visit and why they fascinate you.
Name a natural wonder or landmark you dream of seeing in person.
Write down an adventurous activity or sport you want to try, such as scuba diving or bungee jumping.

_____

_____

_____

_____

_____

_____

_____

_____

_____

_____

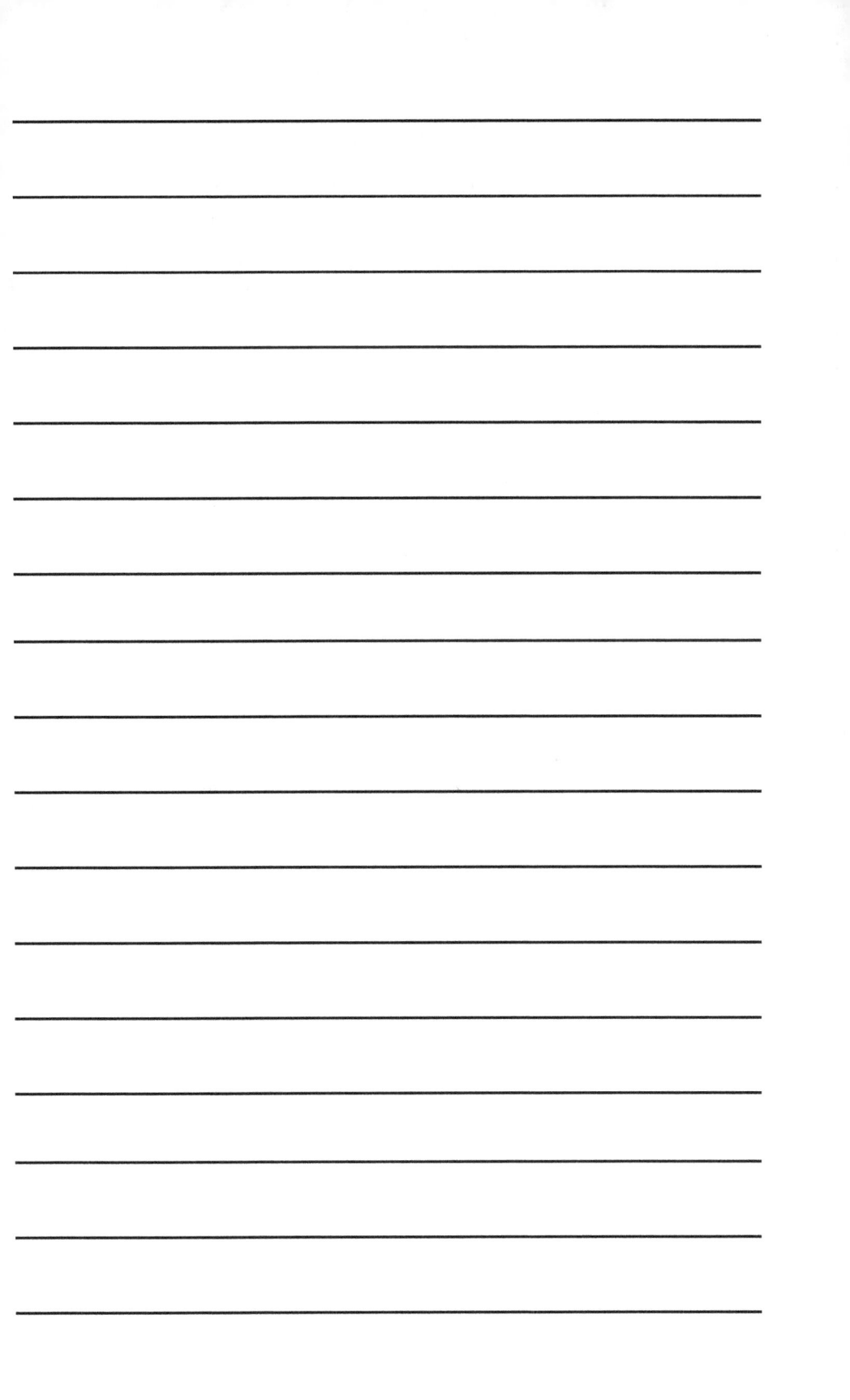

Guide:

Learning and Personal Growth:

Identify a new skill you want to learn, like playing an instrument or cooking a specific cuisine.
List a subject or topic you want to study in-depth and the resources you'll use to do so.
Name a book you've always wanted to read, and commit to finishing it within a specific timeframe.

_____

_____

_____

_____

_____

_____

_____

_____

_____

_____

_____

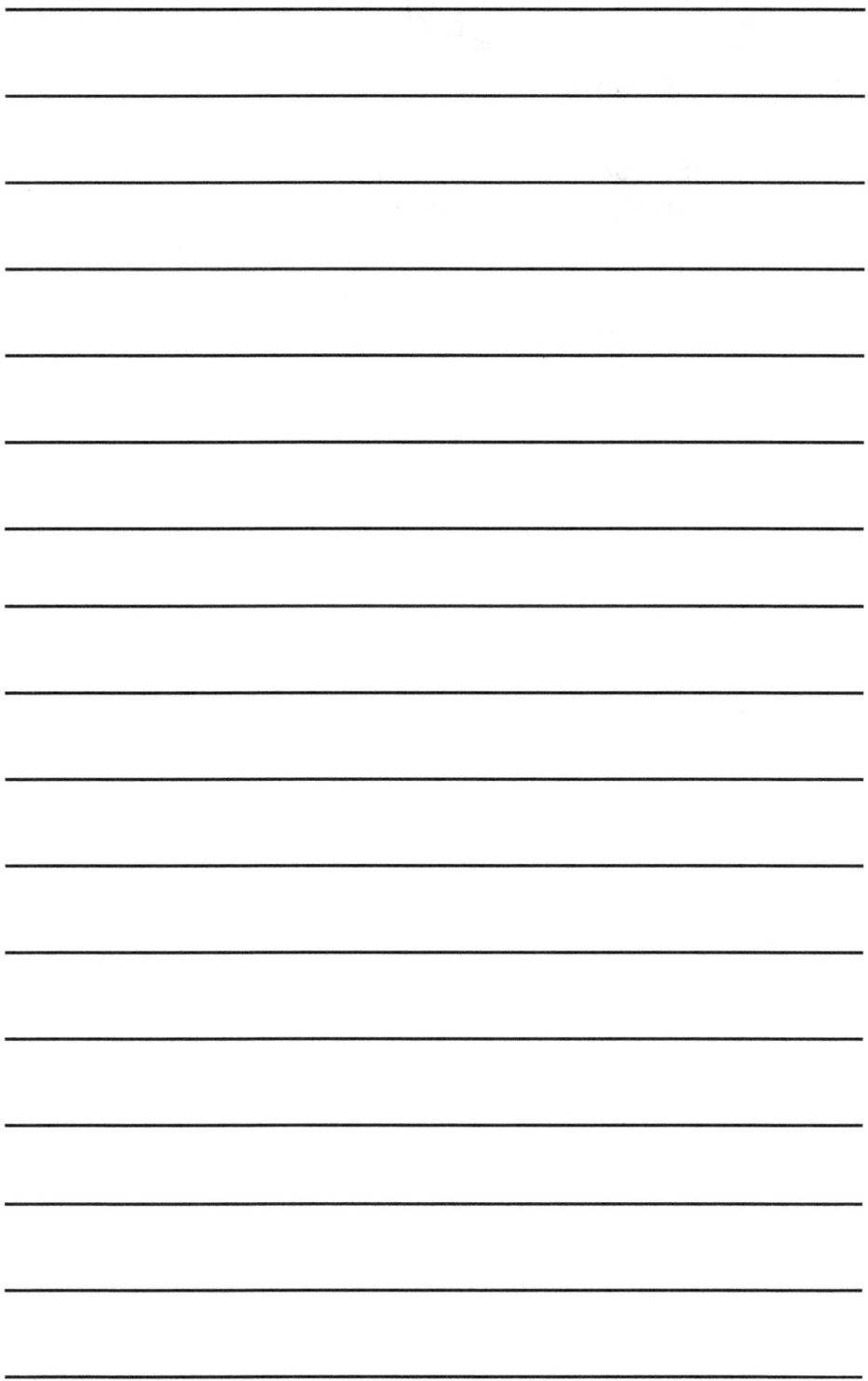

Guide:

Fitness and Health:

Set a fitness goal, such as completing a certain number of push-ups or running a 5K race.
Write down a healthy habit you want to cultivate, like practicing yoga or meditating daily.
Name a challenging outdoor activity you want to conquer, such as hiking a mountain trail.

_____

_____

_____

_____

_____

_____

_____

_____

_____

_____

_____

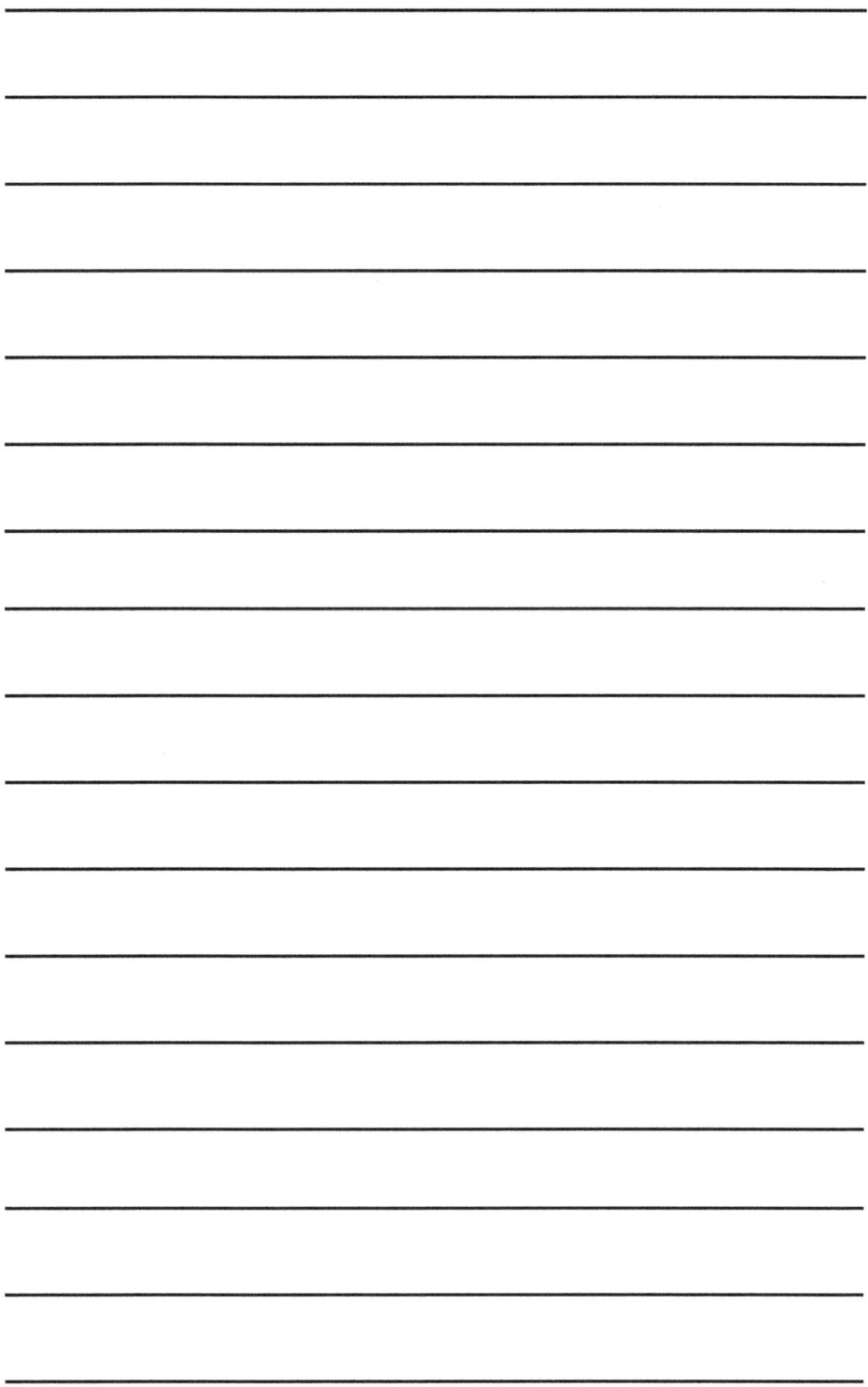

Guide:

Relationships and Connections:

Plan a meaningful reunion or gathering with loved
ones when the time allows.
Write a letter expressing gratitude and love to
someone who has had a significant impact on your life.
List activities or experiences you want to share with
family or friends to strengthen your bond.

_____

_____

_____

_____

_____

_____

_____

_____

_____

_____

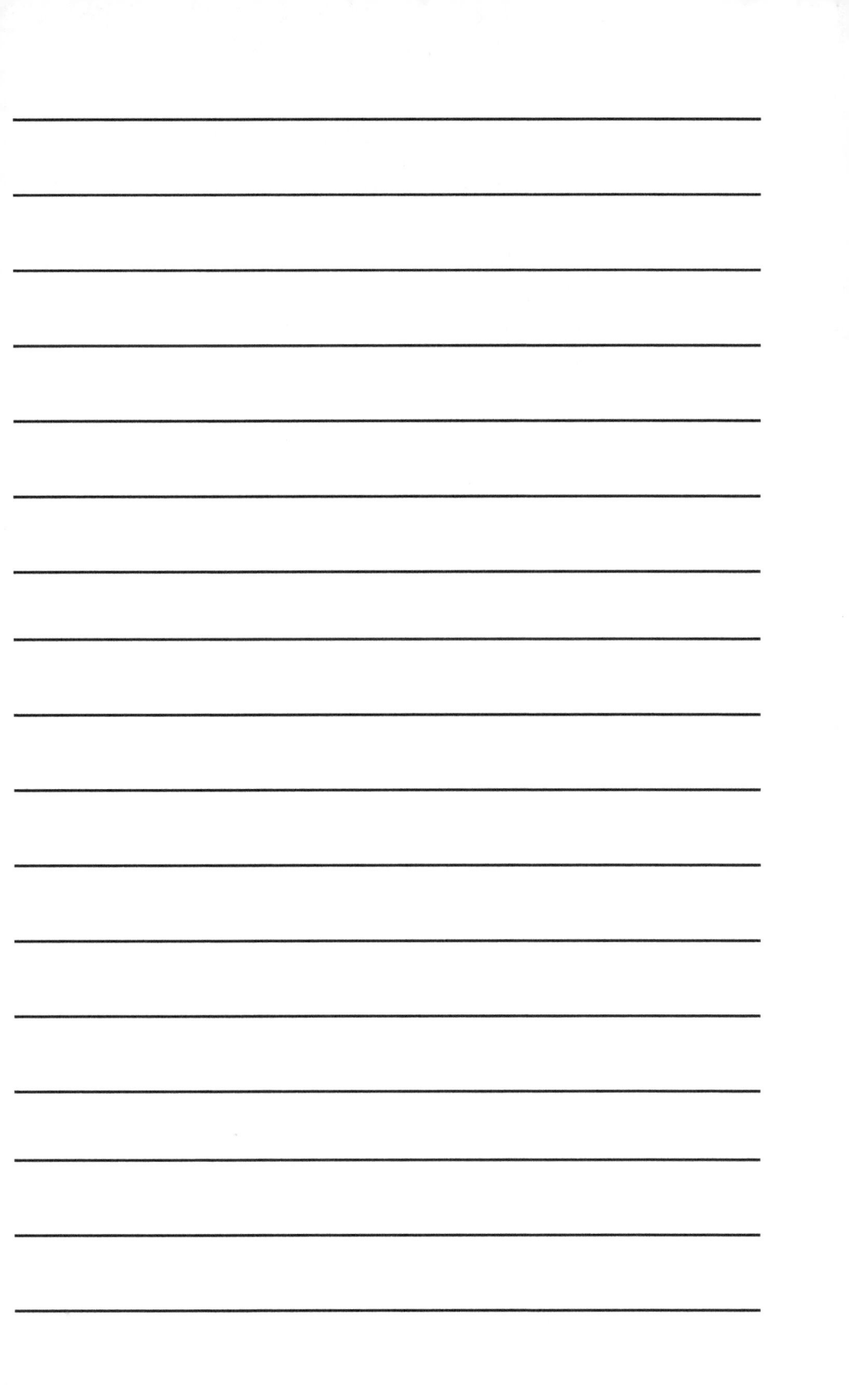

Guide:

Giving Back and Helping Others:

Identify a cause or charity you'd like to support
through volunteering or fundraising efforts.
Write down a creative way to give back to your
community, such as organizing a workshop or event.
List small acts of kindness you can perform regularly
to brighten someone's day.

_____

_____

_____

_____

_____

_____

_____

_____

_____

_____

_____

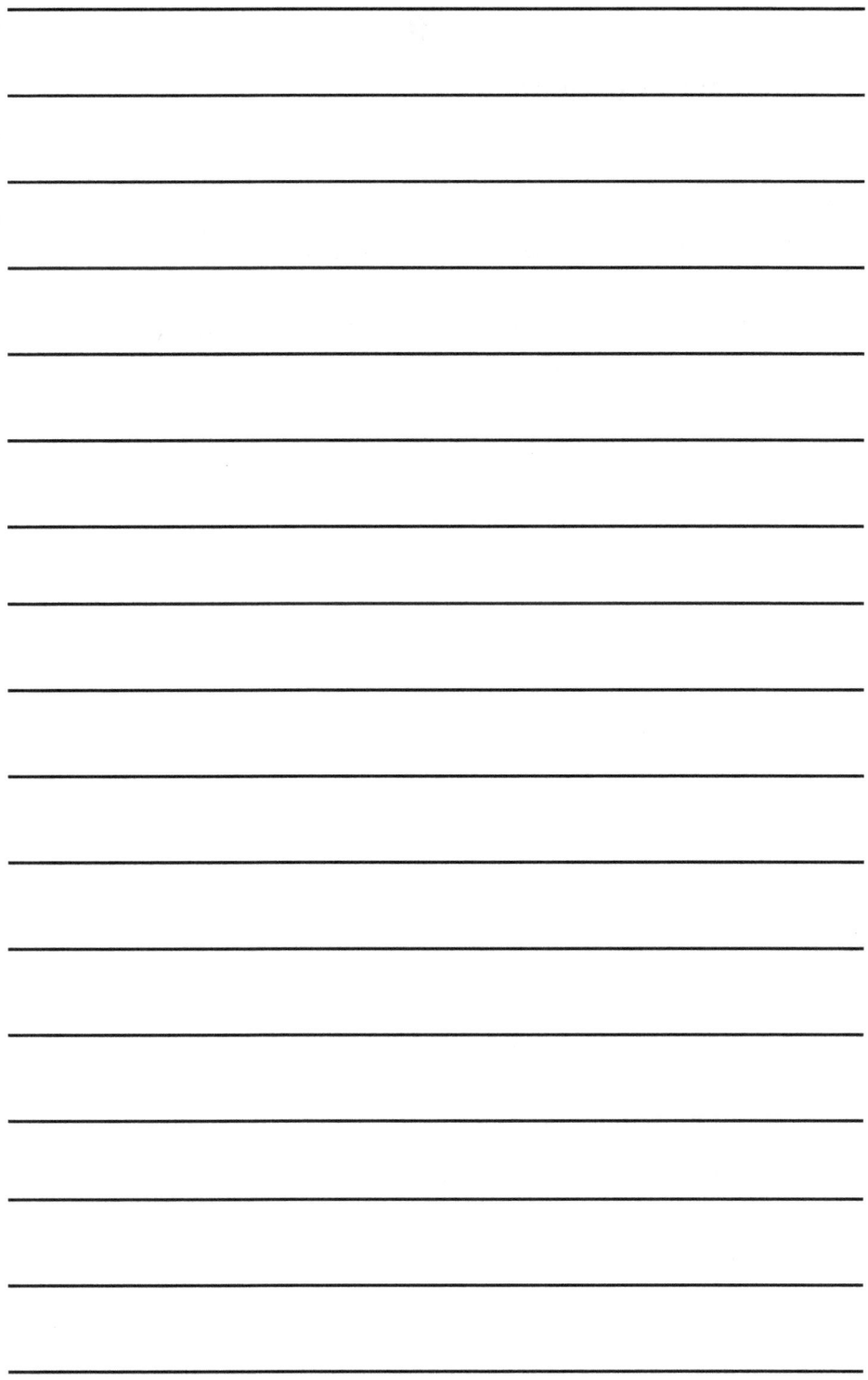

Guide:

Overcoming Challenges:

Name a fear you want to conquer and a plan to face it with courage.
Write down steps to overcome a personal challenge you've been struggling with.
Set a goal related to rehabilitation or personal growth that aligns with your future plans.

_____

_____

_____

_____

_____

_____

_____

_____

_____

_____

_____

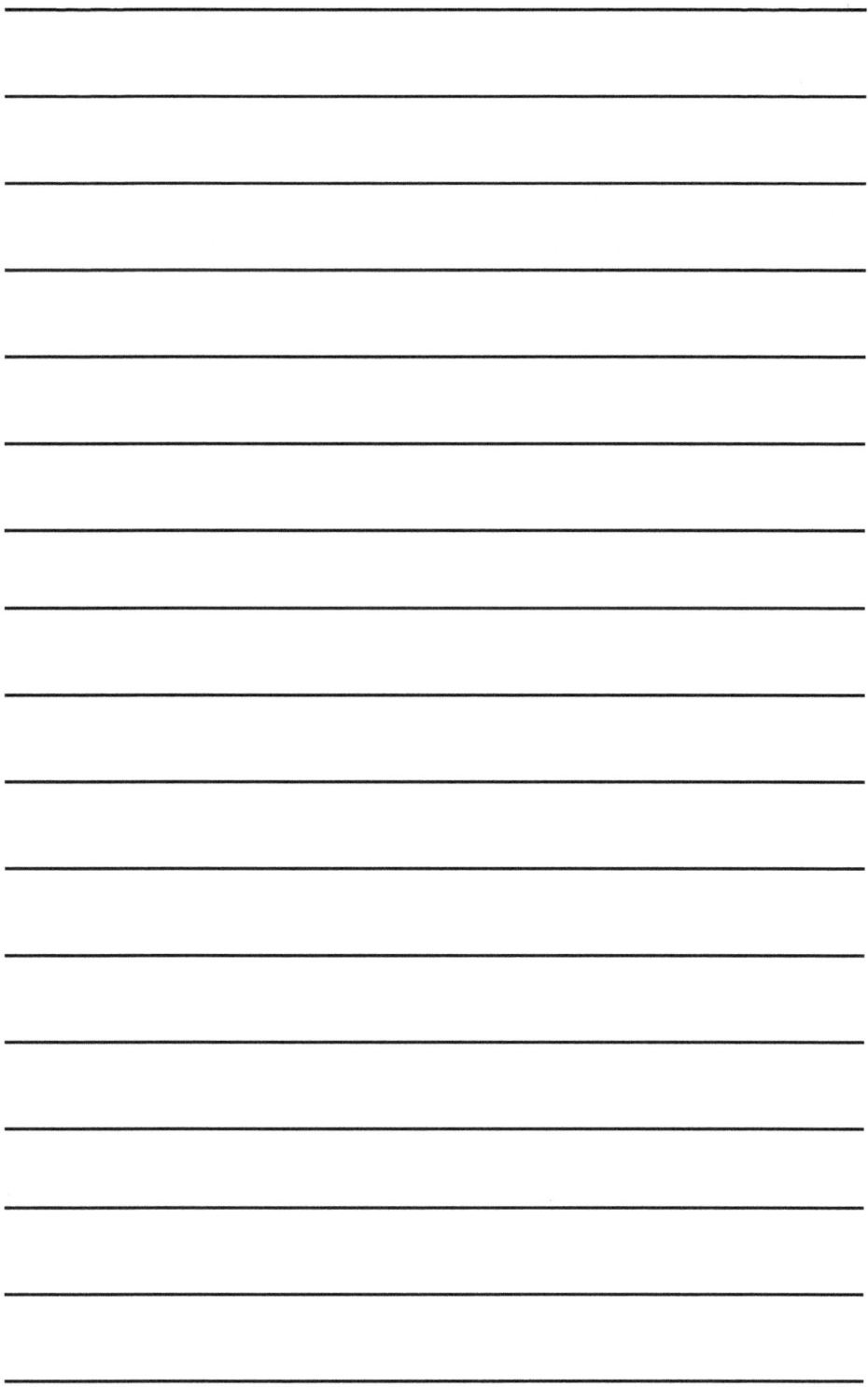

Guide:

Future Planning:

List career or educational goals you want to achieve after your release.
Write down financial goals, like saving a specific amount or investing in a new skillset.
Identify a dream you have for your life after your time in prison, and envision its realization.

_____

_____

_____

_____

_____

_____

_____

_____

_____

_____

_____

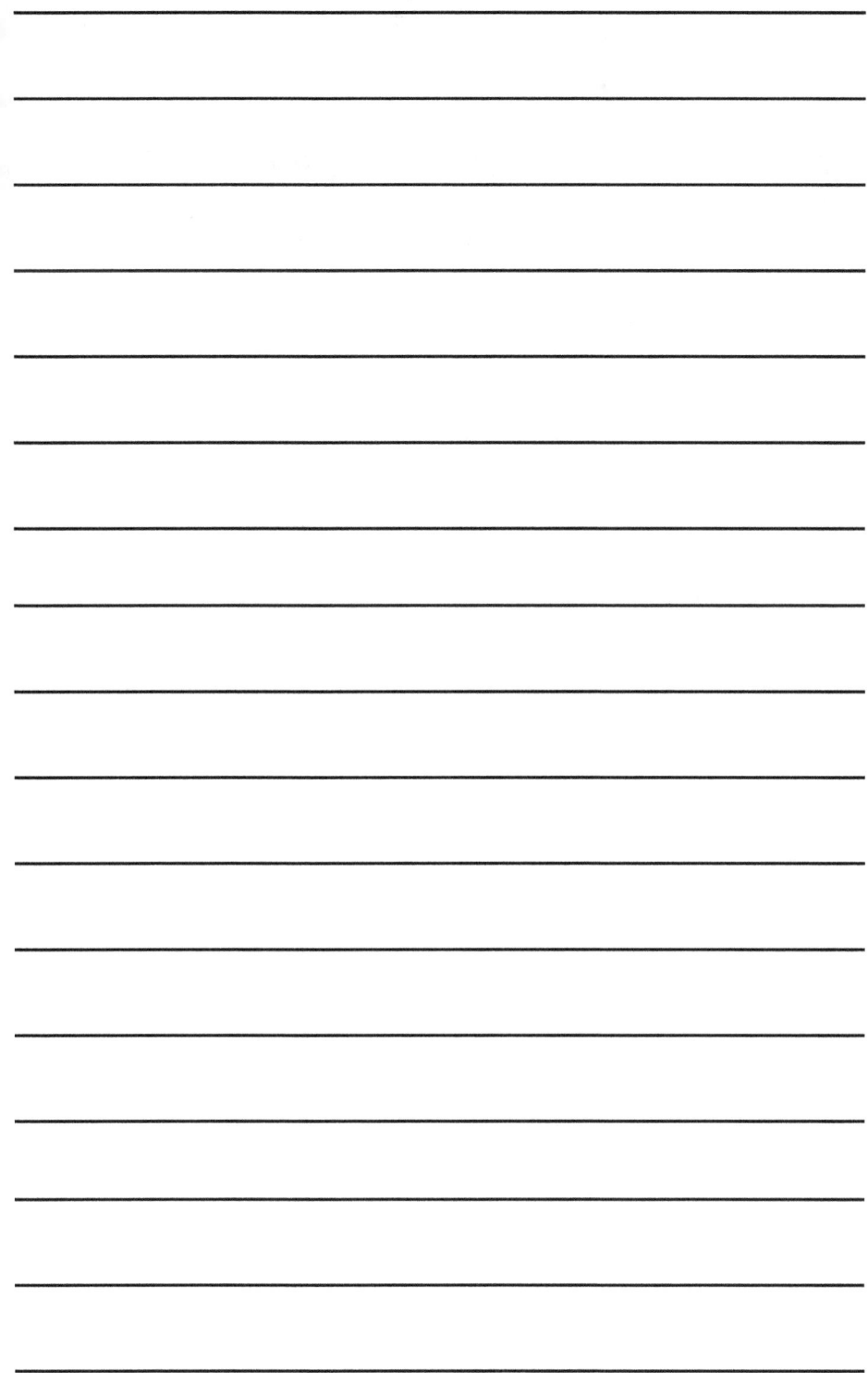

Guide:

Simple Pleasures and Moments of Joy:

Write down simple things that bring you joy, like stargazing or watching a sunrise.
List hobbies or activities that you can enjoy regularly, even within the confines of prison.
Identify moments of laughter and connection you want to cherish with your loved ones.

_____

_____

_____

_____

_____

_____

_____

_____

_____

_____

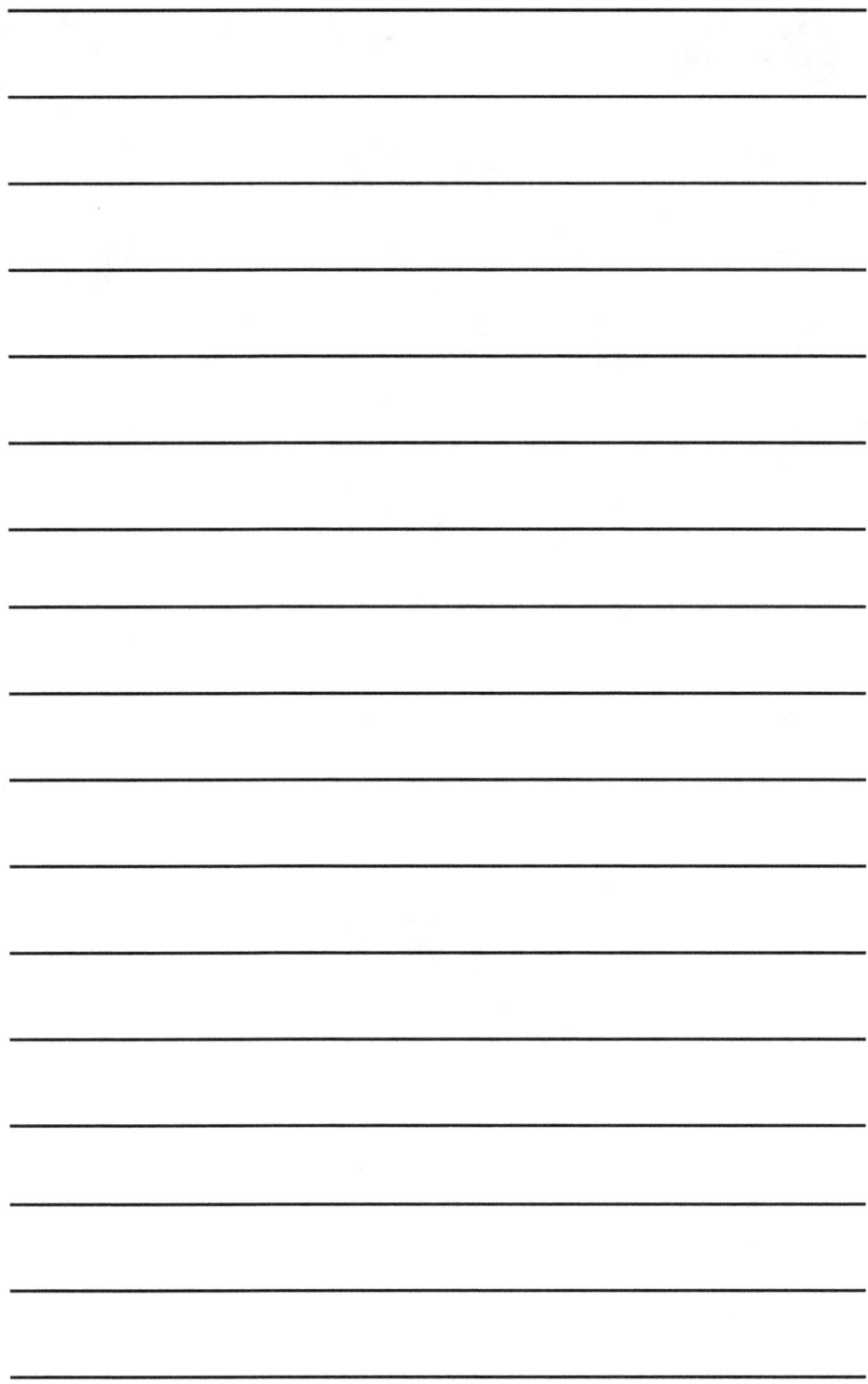

"YOUR PRESENT CIRCUMSTANCES DON'T DETERMINE WHERE YOU CAN GO; THEY MERELY DETERMINE WHERE YOU START." - NIDO QUBEIN

"THE FUTURE BELONGS TO THOSE WHO BELIEVE IN THE BEAUTY OF THEIR DREAMS." - ELEANOR ROOSEVELT

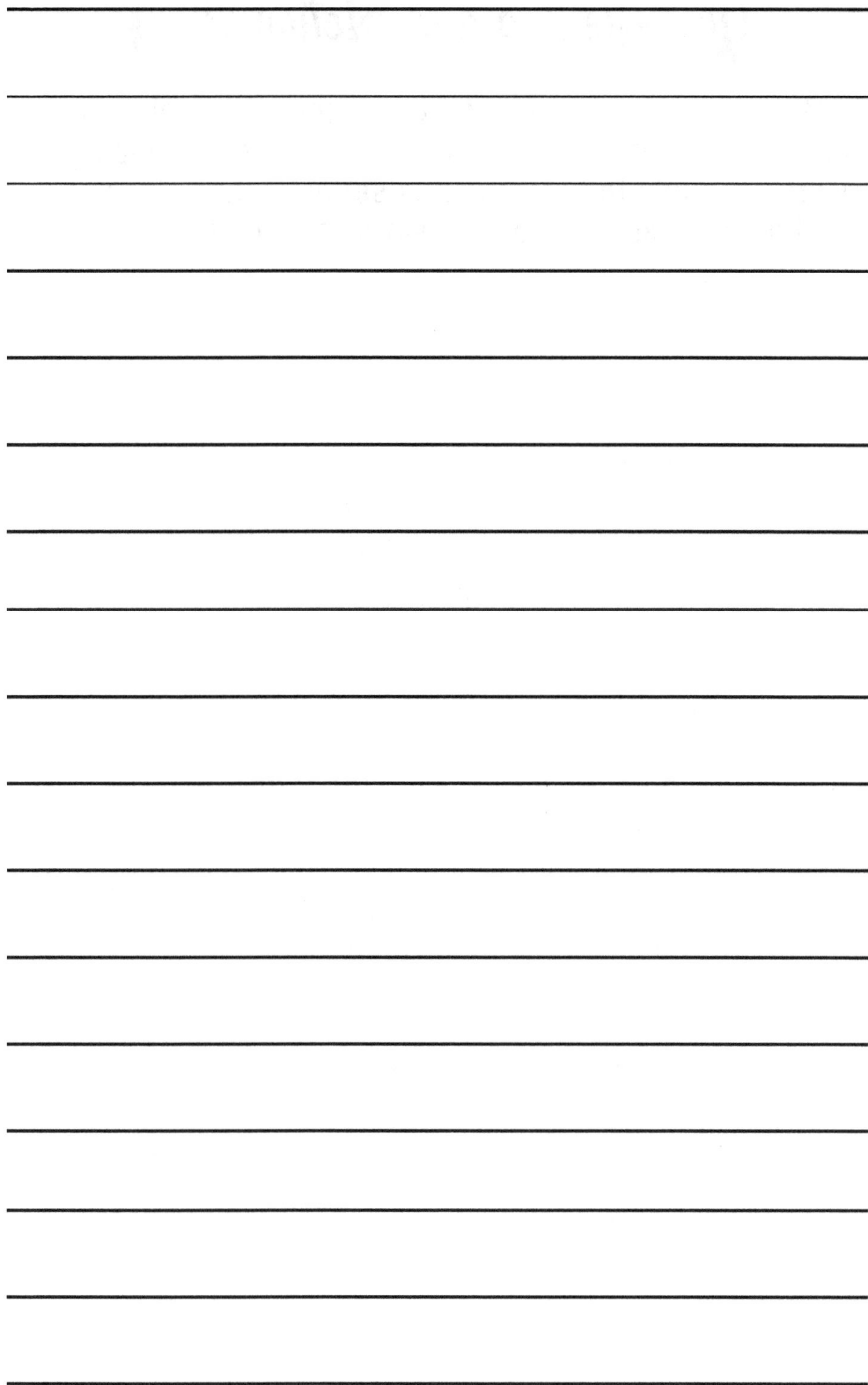

Goal-Setting and Action Plans

Setting achievable goals and creating action plans are essential steps to turn bucket list dreams into reality. Here's a guide to help inmates set meaningful goals and develop action plans to work towards their aspirations:

Step 1: Identify Your Goals

Review your bucket list and identify the most important goals you want to achieve.
Prioritize your goals based on their significance and the level of excitement they bring.

Step 2: Make Your Goals Specific and Measurable

Clearly define each goal in specific terms. For example, instead of "Travel more," specify "Visit Paris and explore its famous landmarks."
Ensure your goals are measurable, so you can track progress and celebrate achievements.

Step 3: Set Realistic and Time-Bound Goals

Make sure your goals are achievable within your resources and capabilities.
Assign a realistic timeline for each goal. It could be days, weeks, months, or even years, depending on the complexity.

Goal-Setting and Action Plans

Step 4: Break Down Goals into Smaller Steps

Divide each goal into smaller, manageable steps or milestones.
Create a timeline for completing these steps to stay on track.

Step 5: Create Action Plans

Develop a detailed action plan for each goal, outlining the steps you need to take.
Include necessary resources, contacts, and research required to achieve your goals.

Step 6: Stay Accountable and Track Progress

Regularly review your action plans and track your progress towards each goal.
Celebrate milestones achieved, and if you face setbacks, reevaluate and adjust your plans accordingly.

Step 7: Seek Support and Encouragement

Share your goals with trusted friends or family who can support and encourage you on your journey.
Engage with positive and like-minded individuals who share similar interests.

Goal-Setting and Action Plans

Step 8: Embrace Flexibility and Adaptability

Life may present unexpected challenges or opportunities. Stay flexible and be willing to adapt your plans when needed.
Remember that your bucket list is a dynamic document; it can evolve as you grow and change.

Step 9: Stay Positive and Motivated

Cultivate a positive mindset and stay motivated even when faced with obstacles.
Visualize the fulfillment of your goals, and let that vision drive your determination.

Step 10: Celebrate Achievements

Celebrate every accomplishment, no matter how big or small.
Take time to reflect on your journey, acknowledging the growth and learning that comes with pursuing your dreams.

Remember, setting goals and creating action plans are powerful tools for turning dreams into realities. Embrace the process with enthusiasm and dedication, knowing that each step you take brings you closer to the life you desire. Your bucket list is an invitation to a life of purpose, joy, and fulfillment. Embrace it wholeheartedly, and let it guide you on an extraordinary journey of self-discovery and growth.

Example

Goal: Learn to Play the Guitar

Step 1: Set a Specific Goal

Clearly define the goal: Learn to play the guitar proficiently.

Step 2: Set a Deadline

Deadline: Within six months from today.

Step 3: Break Down the Goal into Smaller Steps

a) Research and Choose a Guitar:
- Research different types of guitars (acoustic, electric) and their features.
- Visit music stores or online shops to compare options and choose a guitar that suits your preferences and budget.

b) Find a Guitar Teacher or Online Course:
- Look for local guitar teachers or reputable online guitar courses.
- Read reviews and testimonials to ensure the chosen teacher or course is suitable for your learning style.

c) Set Regular Practice Schedule:
- Commit to practicing the guitar for at least 30 minutes every day.
- Create a weekly practice schedule, allocating specific time slots for practice sessions.

Example

d) Learn Basic Chords and Strumming Patterns:
- Start with basic chords such as C, G, D, A, and E.
- Practice transitioning between these chords smoothly.
- Learn simple strumming patterns to accompany the chords.

e) Learn to Play Songs:
- Choose a few songs that you enjoy and have chords suitable for beginners.
- Start with easy songs and gradually progress to more challenging ones.

f) Seek Feedback and Guidance:
- Play for friends, family, or fellow inmates who are supportive.
- Seek constructive feedback and guidance to improve your playing.

g) Join a Guitar Enthusiast Group or Jam Session:
- Look for fellow guitar enthusiasts or join a music group within the facility.
- Participate in jam sessions to gain confidence and experience playing with others.

Step 4: Set Milestones

Milestone 1 (2 weeks): Purchase a guitar and find a suitable teacher or online course.
Milestone 2 (1 month): Learn and practice basic chords and strumming patterns.

Example

Milestone 3 (3 months): Play at least three songs confidently.
Milestone 4 (6 months): Perform a song in front of a small audience.

Step 5: Monitor Progress and Adjust

Regularly track your progress and assess if you're meeting the milestones.
Adjust your practice schedule or seek additional guidance if you encounter challenges.

Step 6: Stay Positive and Motivated

Celebrate each small achievement and milestone.
Stay motivated by visualizing yourself playing the guitar proficiently.

Step 7: Reflect and Learn

Reflect on your journey and the improvements you've made.
Identify areas for further growth and set new goals for your guitar playing.

Remember, breaking down your goals into smaller steps helps you stay focused, organized, and motivated on your path to achievement. Celebrate each step you take and remember that progress is a journey, not a destination. Stay committed to your goal, and the joy of playing the guitar will become a beautiful part of your life.

"YOU ARE
NEVER TOO
OLD TO SET
ANOTHER
GOAL OR TO
DREAM A
NEW DREAM."
- C.S. LEWIS

"EVERY STRIKE BRINGS ME CLOSER TO THE NEXT HOME RUN." - BABE RUTH

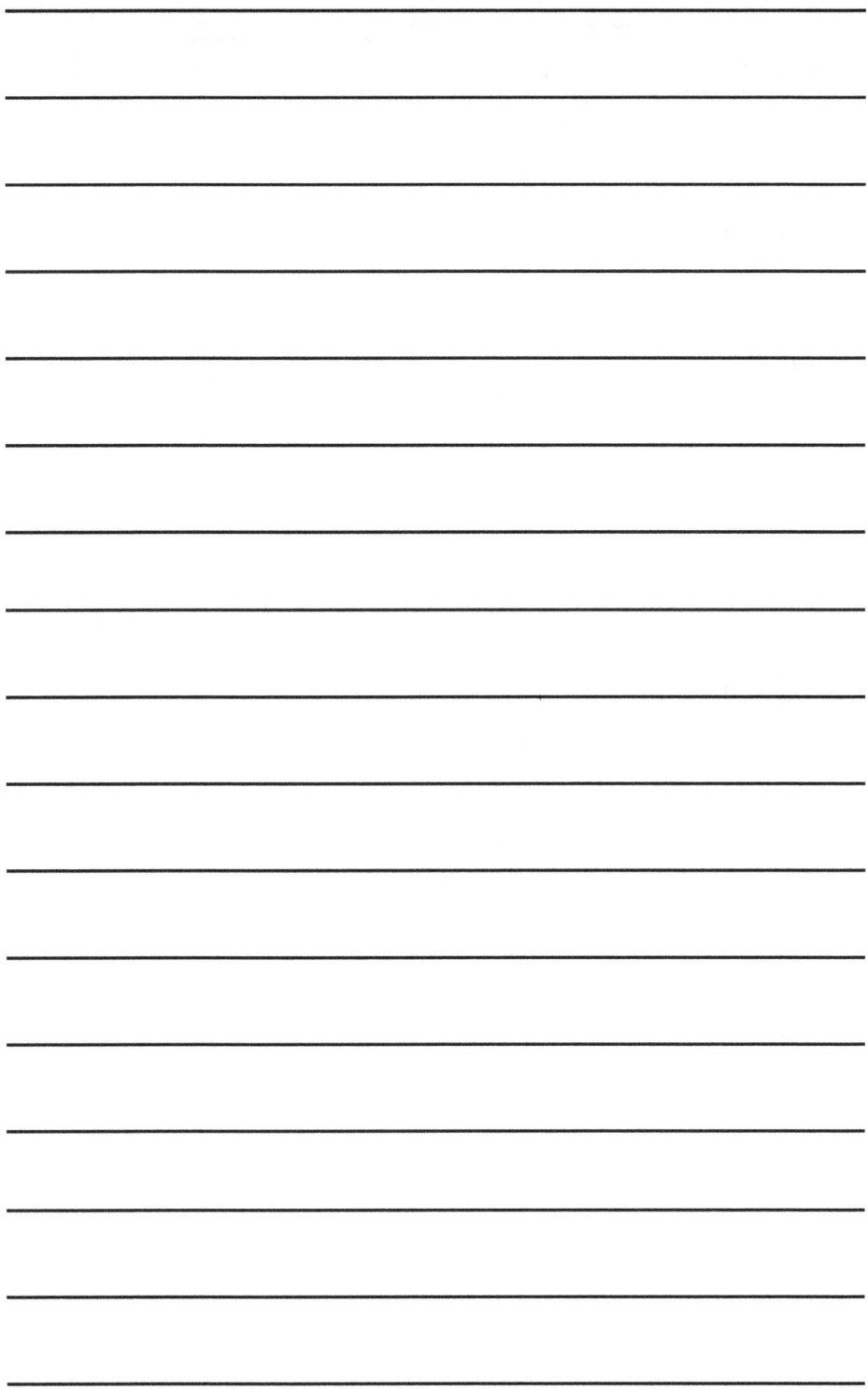

"YOUR TIME IS LIMITED, DON'T WASTE IT LIVING SOMEONE ELSE'S LIFE." - STEVE JOBS

"THE BEST WAY TO PREDICT THE FUTURE IS TO CREATE IT." - PETER DRUCKER

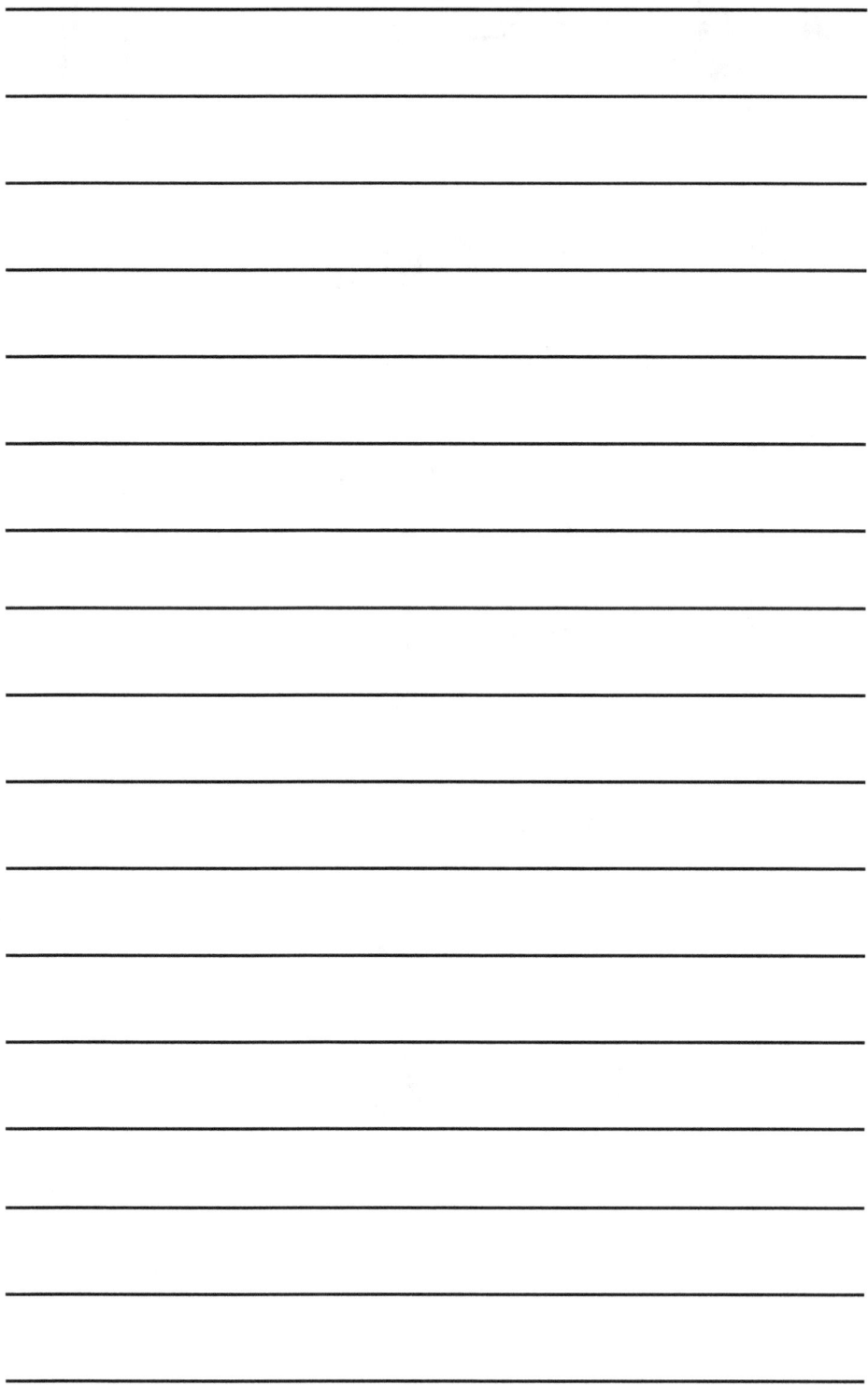

"DON'T WATCH THE CLOCK; DO WHAT IT DOES. KEEP GOING." - SAM LEVENSON

"IN THE
MIDDLE OF
DIFFICULTY
LIES
OPPORTUNITY
." - ALBERT
EINSTEIN

The Journey So Far

Welcome to the "Journey So Far" section of the journal. Here, you have the opportunity to reflect on the progress you've made and the experiences you've had while pursuing your bucket list goals. Each completed item is a testament to your determination, resilience, and the power of your dreams.

Take a moment to celebrate each achievement and acknowledge the growth that came with pursuing your aspirations. Use these pages to write about the memories you've made and the lessons you've learned along the way. Embrace this space as a sanctuary of gratitude and self-discovery.

As you fill these pages, take time to savor the memories, whether big or small, that each accomplishment brought you. Reflect on the lessons you've learned through overcoming challenges, embracing new experiences, and pushing your boundaries.

Use this space to express gratitude to those who supported you along the way and to acknowledge the strength and resilience you've demonstrated. Celebrate your growth, both as an individual and as someone striving to achieve their dreams.

The Journey So Far

Remember that this journal is a testament to the beautiful journey you're embarking on, where every step, every dream achieved, and every experience brings you closer to the person you aspire to become.

May these "Journey So Far" pages serve as a reminder of the incredible potential within you. As you look back on your progress, let it inspire you to continue moving forward, bravely and passionately, on the path to realizing your dreams.

With excitement and anticipation,

The Journey So Far

Bucket List Item Completed:

Date Accomplished:

Reflections:

_____

_____

_____

_____

_____

_____

_____

_____

_____

_____

_____

_____

The Journey So Far

Bucket List Item Completed:
Date Accomplished:

Reflections:

_____

_____

_____

_____

_____

_____

_____

_____

_____

_____

_____

_____

_____

The Journey So Far

Bucket List Item Completed:

Date Accomplished:

Reflections:

_____

_____

_____

_____

_____

_____

_____

_____

_____

_____

_____

The Journey So Far

Bucket List Item Completed:
Date Accomplished:

Reflections:

_____

_____

_____

_____

_____

_____

_____

_____

_____

_____

_____

_____

The Journey So Far

Bucket List Item Completed:

Date Accomplished:

Reflections:

_____

_____

_____

_____

_____

_____

_____

_____

_____

_____

_____

_____

_____

The Journey So Far

Bucket List Item Completed:
Date Accomplished:

Reflections:

_____

_____

_____

_____

_____

_____

_____

_____

_____

_____

_____

_____

_____

The Journey So Far

Bucket List Item Completed:

Date Accomplished:

Reflections:

_____

_____

_____

_____

_____

_____

_____

_____

_____

_____

_____

_____

_____

The Journey So Far

Bucket List Item Completed:

Date Accomplished:

Reflections:

_____

_____

_____

_____

_____

_____

_____

_____

_____

_____

_____

_____

_____

The Journey So Far

Bucket List Item Completed:

Date Accomplished:

Reflections:

_____

_____

_____

_____

_____

_____

_____

_____

_____

_____

_____

_____

_____

The Journey So Far

Bucket List Item Completed:
Date Accomplished:

Reflections:

_____

_____

_____

_____

_____

_____

_____

_____

_____

_____

_____

_____

_____

_____

_____

"THE
JOURNEY OF
A THOUSAND
MILES BEGINS
WITH A
SINGLE
STEP."
- LAO TZU

"SUCCESS IS NOT FINAL, FAILURE IS NOT FATAL: IT IS THE COURAGE TO CONTINUE THAT COUNTS."
- WINSTON CHURCHILL

My Favorite Photos

My Favorite Photos

My Favorite Photos

My Favorite Photos

My Favorite Photos

My Favorite Photos

www.ingramcontent.com/pod-product-compliance
Lightning Source LLC
Chambersburg PA
CBHW070126030426
42335CB00016B/2286